Sports Illustrated KIDS

GAME-CHANGING COACHES

BASEBALL'S BEST
COACHES

Influencers, Leaders, and Winners on the Diamond

written by Nicole A. Mansfield

CAPSTONE PRESS
a capstone imprint

Published by Capstone Press, an imprint of Capstone
1710 Roe Crest Drive, North Mankato, Minnesota 56003
capstonepub.com

Library of Congress Cataloging-in-Publication Data
Names: Mansfield, Nicole A., author.
Title: Baseball's best coaches : influencers, leaders, and winners on the diamond / by Nicole A. Mansfield.
Description: North Mankato, Minnesota : Capstone Press, [2024] | Series: Sports Illustrated Kids: game-changing coaches | Includes bibliographical references and index. | Audience: Ages 8-11 | Audience: Grades 4-6 | Summary: "Sometimes baseball's best player is in the dugout, not on the diamond. Get the details about the best coaches in baseball from college to the pros. Who's got the stats and the championships to be called legend? Who has inspired the most players both on and off the field? Turn these pages to find out!"— Provided by publisher.
Identifiers: LCCN 2023036492 (print) | LCCN 2023036493 (ebook) | ISBN 9781669063476 (hardcover) | ISBN 9781669063605 (paperback) | ISBN 9781669063513 (pdf) | ISBN 9781669063612 (epub) | ISBN 9781669063629 (kindle edition)
Subjects: LCSH: Baseball—Coaching—Juvenile literature. | Baseball coaches—Juvenile literature.
Classification: LCC GV875.5 .M42 2024 (print) | LCC GV875.5 (ebook) | DDC 796.357/2—dc23/eng/20230805
LC record available at https://lccn.loc.gov/2023036492
LC ebook record available at https://lccn.loc.gov/2023036493

Editorial Credits
Editor: Mandy Robbins; Designer: Dina Her; Media Researcher: Jo Miller; Production Specialist: Tori Abraham

Image Credits
Alamy: UPI, 5, Zuma Press, Inc./Darren Eagles/Southcreek Global, 15; Getty Images: Boston Globe, 21, Christian Petersen, 27, Focus On Sport, 25, 28, FPG, 11, GeorgePeters, design element (throughout), George Rinhart, 7, Mitchell Layton, Cover, (bottom left); Library of Congress, 12, 13; MediaNews Group/The Mercury News via Getty Images, 17; Newscom: TSN/Icon SMI 800, 9; Shutterstock: Adam Vilimek, Cover, (middle) background, Dan Thornberg, Cover, (bottom right), Dejan Popovic, Cover, (top left), inspiring.team, Cover, design element (throughout), John Konrad, Cover, (bottom right), Luxury_Studio, design element (throughout), Milano M, Cover, design element (throughout); Sports Illustrated: David E. Klutho, 26, Heinz Kluetmeier, Cover, (top right), John Iacono, 14, 19, Neil Leifer, 8, 22, Peter Read Miller, 20; TopFoto: Chicago History Museum, 10

All internet sites appearing in back matter were available and accurate when this book was sent to press.

TABLE OF CONTENTS

Words in **BOLD** are in the glossary.

GREAT COACHING COUNTS

CRACK! A baseball flies into the stands. It's a home run! Fans love the thrill of professional baseball. They cheer for their favorite teams and players. But sometimes the most valuable player on a Major League Baseball (MLB) team is the coach!

Take Houston Astros manager Dusty Baker. He knows how to handle different types of players. He takes time to teach his players. He is also the first Black MLB manager to win more than 2,000 games.

In 2022, the World Series featured the Astros and the Philadelphia Phillies. Almost 12 million viewers tuned in to watch. In the end, Baker led his team to victory. At the time, he was 73. That made him the oldest manager to win a World Series.

The Astros celebrate their World Series win over the Phillies in 2022.

CHAPTER 1
BACK TO THE BEGINNERS

Some of the best baseball managers were also some of the first. They set the bar high.

Joe McCarthy managed the New York Yankees from 1931 to 1946. McCarthy played in the minor leagues, but he never made it into the majors. He started coaching the pros when he was only in his 20s.

McCarthy was hired in 1926 to manage the Chicago Cubs. In 1931, he became manager of the Yankees. He was a strict coach. He insisted his players dressed and behaved like champions on and off the field. McCarthy was great at developing young players. He had a total of seven World Series wins between 1931 and 1946. McCarthy was elected to the Baseball Hall of Fame in 1957.

McCarthy's "10 Commandments for Success in Baseball"

1. Nobody ever became a ballplayer by walking after a ball.

2. You will never become a .300 hitter unless you take the bat off your shoulder.

3. An outfielder who throws in back of a runner is locking the barn after the horse is stolen.

4. Keep your head up and you may not have to keep it down.

5. When you start to slide, SLIDE. He who changes his mind may have to change a good leg for a bad one.

6. Do not alibi on bad hops. Anyone can field the good ones.

7. Always run them out. You never can tell.

8. Do not quit.

9. Try not to find too much fault with the umpires. You cannot expect them to be as perfect as you are.

10. A pitcher who hasn't control hasn't anything.

Casey Stengel chats with Baltimore Orioles manager Paul Richards.

Casey Stengel led the Yankees from 1949 to 1960. Stengel was famous for his sense of humor. He once told his players to line up alphabetically according to their heights. His humor helped him relate to his players. But Stengel was serious about setting records. He accomplished a **feat** that has yet to be matched. From 1949 to 1953, his team won five World Series in a row.

Casey Stengel and Joe McCarthy are tied as the most successful World Series managers of all time. Both men led the New York Yankees. Both won the World Series a whopping seven times.

Casey Stengel talks to his team at spring training in 1950.

Frank Selee never played in the major leagues. But in 1884, he raised $1,000, quit his job at a watch factory, and bought a minor league team. Selee built his team by recruiting young, average players and coaching them to stardom.

Selee's reputation as a smart manager traveled quickly. In 1890, he got his first shot at coaching in the majors with the Boston Beaneaters. By 1902, he took over as manager of the Chicago Cubs.

Frank Selee

Mordecai Brown

Selee saw a future star in Mordecai Brown. He was nicknamed "Three-Finger" Brown due to an injury. Few managers would have taken a chance on him. Selee knew the injury made his curveball special. Brown became a starting pitcher for the Cubs. Selee was elected to the Baseball Hall of Fame in 1999.

Fact

The $1,000 that Selee raised in 1884 would be more than $31,000 today! But now a minor league team costs between $600,000 and $20,000,000!

Philadelphia Athletics manager Connie Mack began coaching the team in 1901. Mack always wore a suit during games instead of the traditional team uniform. Many managers are loud and aggressive. But Mack was kind and respectful with his players. He never scolded a player in public. He insisted that he got better results that way.

Connie Mack (left)

Mack managed 7,755 games in his career. His record of 3,731 wins has yet to be broken. Mack won nine league championships and five World Series. In 1937, he was elected to the Hall of Fame while he was still coaching.

Connie Mack (right)

Fact

Mack coached the Athletics for 50 years. After 120 years, he still holds the record for longest management of the same team in MLB history!

CHAPTER 2
BREAKING BARRIERS

When professional baseball began, it was a sport dominated by white men. Over time, talented players and coaches have broken that barrier. They have proven that skin color and gender aren't what make someone successful.

Cito Gaston was the first Black American manager to win a World Series. He won two in a row with the Toronto Blue Jays in 1992 and 1993.

Cito Gaston

Catcher John Buck high-fives Cito Gaston during a 2010 Blue Jays game.

Gaston became a hitting coach for the Toronto Blue Jays in 1982. He took over as manager in 1989. Gaston is known as a players' manager. He has always cared about his athletes. He also gave them credit for their hard work. When he **retired**, he made it clear that he could not have enjoyed the success he had without his players.

Alyssa Nakken was the first full-time female coach in Major League Baseball history. She played first base for Sacramento State's softball team from 2009 to 2012. She worked as an intern for the San Francisco Giants while earning her master's degree in sports management. In 2015, Nakken was hired in a non-coaching position by the Giants. She was made a full-time assistant coach in 2020. Nakken got this promotion after earning her master's degree.

Nakken continued to break barriers. In the MLB, only two coaches are allowed to be on the field when their team is batting. On July 20, 2020, she coached at first base during a Giants MLB **exhibition** game. That made her the first female on-field coach in an MLB game. The jersey that she wore that day (#92) was retired and sent to the National Baseball Hall of Fame.

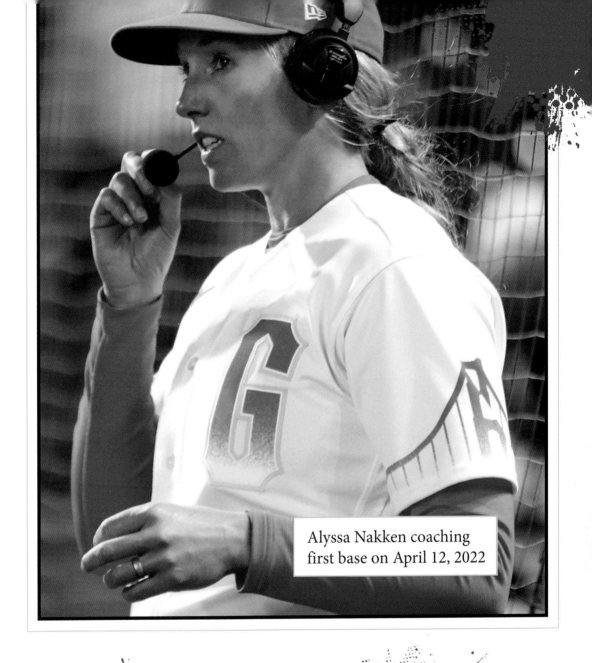

Alyssa Nakken coaching first base on April 12, 2022

Fact

On April 12, 2022, Nakken became the first female ever to coach during a regular season MLB game!

BIG WINNERS AND BIGGER PERSONALITIES

The best managers win lots of games. But some coaches' big personalities are just as impressive as their winning records.

Tommy Lasorda is a Los Angeles Dodgers **legend**. He led them to two World Series championships. Lasorda also helped them rack up 1,599 wins and four National League **pennants**.

Lasorda spent most of his playing career with the Brooklyn Dodgers. In 1973, he became the L.A. Dodgers third base coach. Just three years later, he took over as manager of the team. He was known as an enthusiastic and encouraging manager. He would stick around for hours after practice pitching balls to players who were perfecting their hitting!

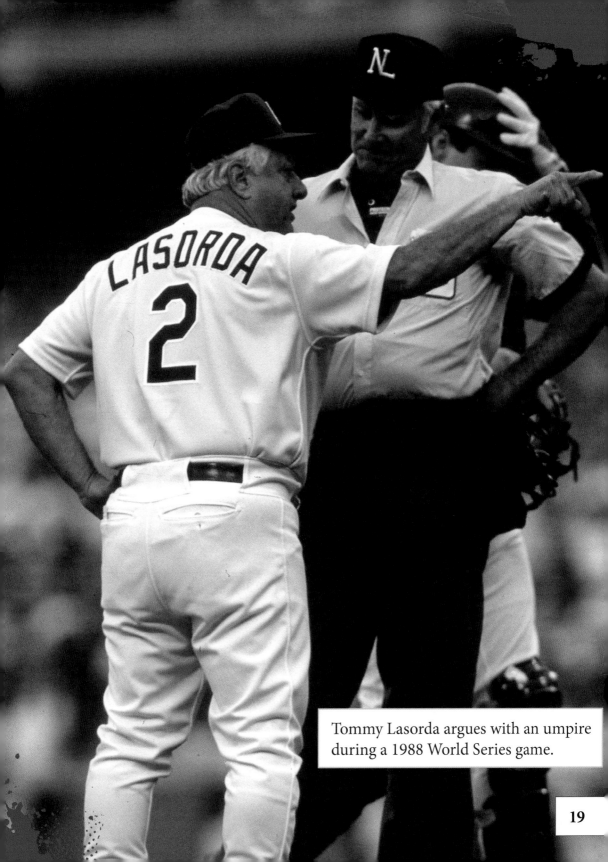

Tommy Lasorda argues with an umpire during a 1988 World Series game.

Lasorda won plenty of ball games, but he also won the hearts of his players and fans. When his team won, he would jump up and down and hug his players. His outspoken, intense personality made him a natural attraction to the public as well. He never held back during interviews. He spoke to his fans, took pictures, and claimed that he bled Dodger blue!

Tommy Lasorda signs a baseball for a young fan.

Lasorda stayed with the Dodgers until the end of his career. He retired on July 29, 1996. He was **inducted** into the Hall of Fame in 1997.

Fact

Tommy Lasorda coached the U.S. Olympic Baseball Team in 2000 in Sydney, Australia. They won the gold medal!

Billy Martin argues with an umpire during a 1976 Yankees game.

Billy Martin started as an aggressive player for the Yankees in the 1950s. He was willing to do anything to win.

Martin started coaching with the Minnesota Twins in 1965. He turned the struggling team around. But Martin's will to win came with a hot temper. He didn't hold back with players, owners, or umpires. Despite his winning record, the Twins fired him in 1969.

Billy moved on to the Detroit Tigers. He made them division winners after just two years but was fired due to his gruff style. Next it was on to the Texas Rangers. He took the last-place team to second place before being fired again.

Martin went back to the Yankees in 1975. They hired and fired him several times before Martin moved on to the Oakland A's. He turned a last-place team into league leaders before ending up back with the Yankees. He managed there on and off again until 1988.

CHAPTER 4
BEST ALL-AROUND

Tony La Russa came to Major League Baseball as a player in 1963 for the Kansas City A's. But he never made it far in the big leagues.

La Russa's career as a manager began with the Chicago White Sox in 1979. At age 34, he was the youngest manager in the league at the time. He had talented players, but his strong suit was getting them to play together as a team. In 1983, he coached the White Sox to 99 wins! La Russa was named American League Manager of the Year for the first time that year. He won the award again in 1988 and 1992.

In 1986, La Russa moved on to the Oakland Athletics. There, he led the A's to three American League Championships in a row! They competed in the World Series in 1988, 1989, and 1990. In 1989, the A's won!

Tony La Russa

La Russa became the manager of the St. Louis Cardinals in 1996. Again, he led his team to become the league champions an astounding three times! This time it was in the National League. In 2006 and 2011, he managed the Cardinals to two World Series wins. He stepped back from managing after that. La Russa went on to serve various roles for the Arizona Diamondbacks and the Boston Red Sox.

In 2021, he came out of retirement to once again manage the White Sox. Health issues sidelined La Russa later that year. Overall, he managed his teams to 2,901 victories. He is second only to Connie Mack for the most wins in MLB history.

Tony La Russa, 2011 World Series

Rod Dedeaux

The greatest coaches in baseball history aren't just in the majors. Rod Dedeaux was head coach of the University of Southern California baseball team for 45 seasons. His teams won 11 College World Series titles with a streak of five years in a row! Dedeaux was voted Coach of the **Century** by *Collegiate Baseball* magazine in 1999.

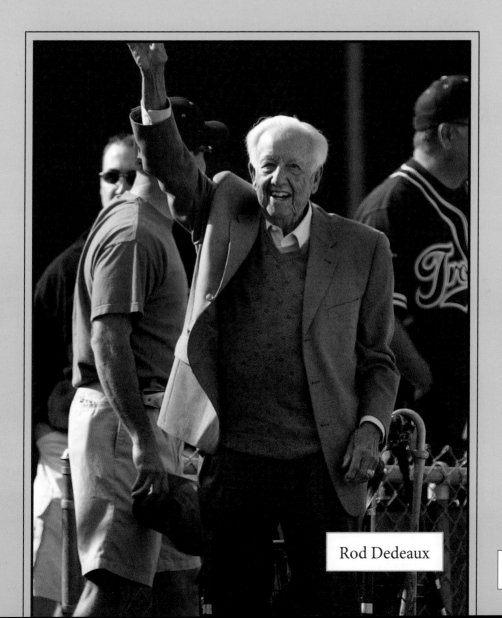

Rod Dedeaux

Few people are the best at every part of the game. Joe Torre is one of them. He is the only person in the MLB to have over 2,000 hits as a player and more than 2,000 wins as a manager! Torre was inducted into the Hall of Fame in 2014.

Torre became an MLB manager in 1977 for the New York Mets. Over 29 seasons, he managed five teams in the majors.

He led the Yankees from 1996 to 2007. Torre's Yankees made the playoffs every year and won six pennants and four World Series under his leadership. The Yankees retired his uniform (#6) in 2014. They honored him with a plaque in Monument Park at Yankee Stadium.

Joe Torre speaks to pitcher Jimmy Key.

TIMELINE

[1884 Frank Selee buys his own minor league team for just $1,000.

[1937 Connie Mack is inducted into the Hall of Fame.

[1957 Joe McCarthy is inducted into the Hall of Fame after compiling seven World Series wins between 1931 and 1946.

[1999 *Collegiate Baseball* magazine votes Rod Dedeaux Coach of the Century.

[2000 The U.S. Olympic Baseball Team wins the gold medal in Sydney, Australia, under Tommy Lasorda's managing.

[2014 The Yankees retire Joe Torre's uniform (#6).

[2022 Almost 12 million viewers watch Houston Astros manager Dusty Baker lead his team to victory in the World Series.

GLOSSARY

CENTURY (SEN-chuh-ree)—a period of 100 years

EXHIBITION (ek-suh-BI-shuhn)—a game played only for show; exhibition games do not count toward the regular season

FEAT (FEET)—an outstanding achievement

INDUCT (in-DUHKT)—to formally admit someone into a position or place of honor

LEGEND (LEJ-uhnd)—a person who is among the best at what he or she does

PENNANT (PEN-uhnt)—a triangular flag that symbolizes a league championship

RETIRE (ri-TIRE)—to give up a line of work

READ MORE

Abdo, Kenny. *History of Baseball*. Minneapolis: Abdo Zoom, 2020.

Berglund, Bruce. *Baseball GOATs: The Greatest Athletes of All Time*. North Mankato, MN: Capstone Press, 2022.

Ciocchi, Catherine. *Science and the Baseball Park*. Louisville, KY: Gnome Road Publishing, 2023.

INTERNET SITES

Five Legendary Baseball Coaches
sports-management-degrees.com/lists/five-legendary-baseball-coaches/

National Baseball Hall of Fame
baseballhall.org

The Best MLB Managers in History
thedelite.com/best-baseball-managers-mlb-history

INDEX

ABOUT THE AUTHOR

Nicole A. Mansfield is a wife, mother, and educator. She dedicates this book to the people who have taught her the most, her family— Connie, Walter, and Cheryl Mills, Justin; Victorious, Justine, and Zion Mansfield. Nicole is passionate about serving at her church and vacationing at the beach!